Table of Contents

Table of Contents

C is for Christmas

Words to Decorate the Holidays

Written by

Thena Smith

Includes Digital Art CD by

Sharon Hammond

Edited by

Bethany Brengan

BP

Bluegrass Publishing Inc
Mayfield, KY
270.251.3600
www.bluegrasspublishing.com

For information write:
Bluegrass Publishing Inc
PO Box 634
Mayfield, KY 42066 USA
service@theultimateword.com
www.bluegrasspublishing.com
www.theultimateword.com

ISBN: 1-59978-003-8

1st ed.
Mayfield, KY : Bluegrass Pub., 2006

Cover Design: Todd Jones, Tennessee
Proudly printed in the United States of America

Dedication

Dedicated to
my Heavenly Father,
from whom I received
the most wonderful gift
of all on that very first Christmas!

About the Book

Some folks have mentioned that they have trouble journaling about Christmas because they always do the same things, eat the same foods and take the same photos -- these customs are called traditions, and they are a great place to begin your journaling! Take the photos and scrap the family tradition. If Dad always carves the turkey, and Aunt Edna always brings the rolls, while Grandpa tells stories about when Dad was young... record that and enjoy it.

With the huge advancement in photography, especially the availability of high resolution digital cameras, many of us have a great abundance of photos, especially holiday photos. We can be selective and creative as we snap the holiday. We can take those photos of the lighted tree, which were once impossible for amateurs to capture. We can capture the look on the children's faces as they are awed by the soft glow of candles. We can get close-up photos of faces and of hands exchanging gifts.

For those of us in the autumn of our lives, we have the advantage of looking back and writing forward. Most of us have photos from past years that we haven't scrapped. We can scrap the photos now, knowing, as we journal, the feelings we had then and the feelings we have now. Things that we once worried about have now been resolved, and we know the outcome. Use this to your advantage.

Younger folks, and especially new moms and dads, have the advantage of the joy, thrill and newness of the moment. You are creating your traditions now. Each of us has a worthy perspective to share.

It is my hope that within the pages of this little book, you will find something to jumpstart your journaling, refresh your memories and cheer you on to share your joy! May it encourage you, inspire you and remind you of the reason for the season!

With Love,

Thena

The SEASON of ADVENT

Advent Calendar for You

This little calendar is special.
It is to guide your thoughts each day
To the special celebration
That comes on Christmas Day.
Advent means "arrival" or "coming,"
That is, the coming of our King.
More than just an historic event,
But a promise for every human being.
Follow along in this little booklet
As you count down each day,
For it will help you to celebrate Christmas
In a very special way.

Advent Calendars

Here's a little calendar with chocolates
To help you on the way
To counting down the time,
Down to the very day,

When Christmas bells will ring
And the holiday is here:
The day that you've been waiting for,
For the whole long year!
For by the time the chocolate's gone...
Christmas will be here!

Delights of December

The Spirit of Advent

This little calendar,
While a lot of fun,
Has a message ~~
A very important one.
It counts down the days
Until the blessed day
When Jesus was born
In a manger far away.
Use it to remind you,
As Christmas you anticipate,
Of the wonderful Advent
That we are going to celebrate!

This Little Calendar

This little calendar
Was created for you
And gives you something
So special to do.

You can use it to count
The days yet to be
Before it is Christmas,
And it will be easy to see.

Turn a page each day
And read what is there,
Ending the day
With a heartfelt prayer.

Countdown to Christmas

CHRISTMAS ALBUMS

Our Special Friends

We wanted to give you something special
To show you how much we care,
Something to celebrate your children
And the love for them that we share.

So we put together this little album,
Showcasing your wonderful little ones,
Full of the routine of family life,
Which makes the holiday such a special one.

You are blessed beyond all measure
With the children God has given you.
And they, along with you, dear friends,
Are a blessing to us too!

Christmas Memories

Our Christmas memories
Are so rare and so sweet:
From decorating the tree
To special things we eat.
We record them each year,
As we celebrate the day,
In photos for our album
For us to replay.

Pictures and Remembrances

Family Christmas Album

Sometimes with our families,
It's hard to impart
All the love and pride
That's in our heart.

Sometimes there seems to be
No words to say
Just how much we love you
And how you bless our day!

Sometimes we do not let our loved ones know,
Hoping that our actions will show
And hoping they will reveal,
Just how blessed and lucky we feel...

Today we want to let you know
Just how special you are to us
And how, each and every day,
Our loving thoughts are sent your way.

As you look through these pages,
I hope that they will help you to see
Just how very special and treasured
Your family is to our family and to me!

Grandmom, I love you!
You are the best
Of all the Grammas
In the whole wide world!
And I'm so lucky
To be your special little girl.

Holiday Memories Warm the Heart

Grandmothers are Special

Grandmothers are special,
Handpicked by God above
To shower blessings on families
And show them His love!
I made a little brag book
For all the world to see
How much I love you, Grandmother,
And how special you are to me!

Grandmom, I love you,
And I know I'm your pride and joy.
And I'm so lucky
To be your special little boy!

Just a little bit of Christmas
To bring your face a smile,
A bit of glittery Christmas fun
To cheer you for awhile.
Enjoy your family and your friends.
And each tradition embrace,
As you make new family memories,
While recording in your heart
The happiness on each face.

The Very Perfect Gramma for a Kid like Me!

Grandparents' Album

I wanted to give you a special gift
That will be a treasure for years to come,
So I created this little album,
And it is a very special one!

On each page you will find,
Created with photos and such,
Remembrances of special times
That I know you treasure so much.

Your grandchildren are all accounted for,
On pages bright and gay,
To bring happiness to your Christmas
And joy for your every day.

You can add to this special album,
As you take photos through the year,
And keep this booklet to remind you
That we hold you very dear!

I will be happy to help you add to it.
Just send the album back to me,
And I will do the pages for you,
Documenting each special memory!

A Christmas Album for You

Here is a little album
That has a great start,
For it was a product
Of love right from my heart.
But it is not yet finished;
There is much more to do,
Pictures and remembrances
To be added throughout the year... by you!

Happy Holidays

A Christmas Album for Our Sister

God may not have seen fit
To make genetic sisters of us all.
But we are connected by threads of love,
With each heart in tune to the other's call.

When one of our sisters hurts,
That hurt we each one feel.
Though it may not be a physical wound,
The hurt in our heart is real.

We have come together in this book
To show you how much we care
And to surround you with our loving thoughts
And keep you lifted up in prayer.

You may not meet us personally,
But this little book will show
That we care so very much for you,
And we just wanted you to know.

Sister,

I love you so much, I cannot express it.
But I felt you should know,
And I ought to confess it:
I opened my present that you sent through the mail.
If that is illegal, will you post my bail?

You Light Up My Life

Another Family Album for Christmas

Family Christmases are special
And stay in our hearts forever.
Every tradition or gathering
Is a wonderful family treasure.

Family from near and far,
Traditions and events,
Vacations in plush hotels,
Or camping out in tents...

All these things are recorded here,
With photographs and stories too ~~
A family album just waiting
For me to share with you!

A Gift Album for Dad

I searched and searched for a gift
Which my love for you would impart,
When all the while the gift was close,
For it was within my heart.

I took the love from this heart of mine
And fond memories of you.
And from those came this special gift,
Made as only love can do.

Home is the Heart of the Holidays

Album for a Special Young Woman

I wanted to give you a special album,
Which can hold treasures for years to come,
So I created this little album just for you,
And it is a very special one!

On each page are special memories
With photos starting when you were young.
Watching you mature and grow
Has been a pleasure and such fun.

Throughout the years you have always had
A special place in my heart.
You were someone extraordinary,
And I felt it from the start.

You have become such a lovely young lady,
So beautiful through and through.
You are such a joy to know,
And I am so very proud of you!

Know that as you go through life,
No matter where you go,
I will always cheer for you.
Just wanted you to know!

I wish you a very special,
Delightful Christmas Day,
Full of all the very best
That God can send your way!

The Best Christmas Gift

You Make Life Special (Mom and Dad)

Thank you, Mom and Dad,
For all that you do.
Life wouldn't be as wonderful,
Were it not for you.

You watch our kids,
While we work all day,
And still invite them
Back over to play.

They treasure your love
And cherish so much
Just being with you
And your special touch!

We put together in this little book
Some special peeks into our world each day.
And with this book is a gaggle of love,
All bundled up and sent your way,
To bring happiness to your Christmas Day!

No One like You

There is absolutely no one like you,
Not only on Christmas,
But the whole year though!
On holidays you add the sparkle,
The rhythm and the shine.
And it makes me so happy
To say that you are mine!

I See the Spirit of Christmas in You

Dear Mom and Dad,

I'm sending you the photos
That we took around the Christmas tree.
They are photos of the kids
And some of hubby and me.

There are photos with the dog
Dressed up in a Santa hat
And some with the youngest one
Using doll clothes to dress the cat.

There are some of you and Dad,
As you hugged the kids that night.
Some we took as we sang Christmas carols
By the glow of candlelight.

These photos are precious to us,
And we will place them in a book.
So that even years from now,
We can open it up and look.

I am writing down the story
Of what we did and said.
The kids love for me to read it
As they prepare to go to bed.

Even though you were with us
Just for the holiday,
With our little family album,
You are a part of our lives each day.

Everyone Smile and Say "Merry Christmas!"

PHOTOS and SCRAPBOOKING

Christmas Photos

I took Christmas photos today,
And when I saw them,
They took my breath away.
For I looked down expecting to see
My children young and babyish,
But you looked back at me,
So grown up and beautiful to see.

I had to briefly look away
From the lovely photos
That I took today.
I had to catch my breath.
And then look back to view
The adorable photos
(So grown up!) of all of you.
I will put them on our Christmas cards
And send them to our friends, and then
I will come back to my desk
And look at them once again.

Christmas Photos Help Us
To Record Each Year
The Changes that Have Happened
When We Weren't Looking!

Timeless Holiday Memories

Christmases Past

Sometimes we look questioningly
On our pages from Christmases past ~~
At holiday memories we caught on film,
So they would always last.

We see friends of family members,
Who are not with us anymore.
We see relatives and neighbors
And other kinfolks by the score.

We see cousins that we know by name,
But see rarely, if at all,
Or some that look familiar,
But whose names we can't recall.

I love to look at photos
And reminisce of times long past.
And I'm thankful for old Christmas cards and photos
That help these memories last.

Our Christmas Photos

Our photos are so special,
Taken 'neath the Christmas tree,
Where family members smile,
As they look up at me.
The tree looks so lovely,
With ornaments so fragile and rare.
And I can almost smell
The aroma of Christmas in the air!

The Christmas Photo

Family Get-Together

When the family gets together,
It is such a happy time.
It makes me really happy
Just to think that they are mine!

Cousins, uncles, aunts and in-laws,
Relatives by the score...
It doesn't matter how many come:
There's always room for more!

And the cameras start to flash
At every cute thing a baby does.
And about the latest teenage craze,
The relatives are all abuzz.

We try to get them all together,
To get a photo of the group.
Some kid is sure to start to cry,
And some kid's got the croup!

Just when we think we have the pose
That will go on next year's Christmas card,
We are distracted by the door bell ringing
Or the dogs barking out in the yard.

So the photos may be fuzzy,
With a few eyes closed and such,
But the memories of those special times
Our hearts will always touch!

Christmas is Filled with Kids & Kisses

Scrapper's Christmas

May all your pages be acid free
With blessing bestowed
From **A to Z**!

May **All** your colors be bright and bold,
Beautiful and **B**lessed, beyond all you know!
May carols that gently filled your ears
Linger in your heart to bless your year.

May your cardstock be appropriate
To the occasion you're scrapping,
And may you find time to create **D**iecuts,
While the children are napping!

May your **E**dges be even
And your ribbons never **F**ray,
Cooperating as you work
Every single day!

May your **G**lue always stick
And your stickers stay sticky.
May you never complete
A page that is icky!

May your **H**ubby support you
And never be a frustration,
May you be able to enjoy
Each scrapping situation!

May **I**deas flood your brain.
May you **J**ournal with care,
And may **K**eepsakes be stashed
With the epitome of flare!

May your **L**ettering be delightful,
Your fonts stylish and true,
And your pages be perfect
To tell folks of you!

May your **M**emories come flooding
Back to your heart,
As you make each page
Into a work of art.

Never look back
To negate what you've done ~~
Enjoy each **O**pportunity presented
To share your memories with fun.

May your ovals be perfect
And your rectangles "right on"
And your pictures **P**erfection ~~
Making you burst into song!

May your **Q**uilt pages be treasured
(And look sweetly homespun)
And your **R**ub-ons stay put,
When the rubbing is done.

May your **S**hoebox of photos
Soon dwindle in size
And your **T**reasury of albums
Bring admiring sighs.

May your "**U**ndo" work quickly,
Your mistakes be gently healed,
And your **V**ellum enhanced **W**ish list
Be lovingly filled.

May your **X**-tra pages fit perfectly
And your **Y**oungsters be cute,
As you **Z**estfully complete albums
And chat and compute!

Merry Scrapping!

CHRISTMAS with FAMILY and FRIENDS

Feel free to change the gender of the poem to fit your needs.

(sister to brother or daughter to son)

Christmas Holds Time Together

Christmas is such a special day,
A precious treasure in every way.
Old and young can appreciate
And come together to celebrate.
The tiny baby, soft and new,
Comes cooing sweetly to snuggle with you.
And grandma, with loving heart,
Has love and wisdom to impart.
Oh, that the whole wide world through
Might be filled with the love and joy
Which I see in you .

We are Family

We are a family,
And we love to be together
When Christmas comes.
We will get home,
No matter what the weather.

We love our big ole family
And consider it priority number one
To be together and celebrate
And have a bit of fun.!

Kids at Christmas

Look at the Christmas tree.
Look at the packages underneath.
Catch a glimpse of a smiling face,
Lighting up like a wreath!

Can you see the kids in the hallway,
Peeking in from the half closed door?
Oh, what delight awaits them tonight!
Could they wish for anything more?

I can't wait until sunlight awakes them,
And they rush down the hallway to see
The gifts that Santa left them
Underneath the Christmas tree!

Teen Christmas

It's not easy being a teen.
When Christmas comes around,
I must go visiting with the family
Or I'm met with a frown.

I don't mean to be disrespectful,
But sometimes relatives are boring,
Especially after Christmas dinner,
When the older ones start snoring!

No Sneakin' and No Peekin'

Christmas Time

Christmas time is a special time
That makes us pause and consider
The loved ones we hold dear.
Some may live far away,
While others may be near.

So know that I am thinking of you,
And I hold you in my heart
On Christmas Day and every day,
Though we may be far apart.

As you celebrate the season,
Pause a moment to remember me
And hang a special little remembrance
On your Christmas tree.

Family Christmas Memories

Years come and go
So very fast,
But Christmas memories
Always last.

Mistletoe and shiny bells
(Hung on tree or post),
Hugs, kisses and teddy bears
Are some memories treasured most.

Christmas comes but once a year
For babies, grandparents, man, or wife,
But the memories created in that time
Last you all of your life.

Christmas Time is Family Time

To My Grandmother

When I think of Christmas Eve,
I look forward to spending it with you.
For in your home we all feel special,
And nowhere else will do.

It is our family tradition,
For your home is filled with joy
That is felt by every mom and dad,
And every girl and boy.

I always loved to open the gifts,
And the fun and stories we share,
But the most important part of all
Is that you were there!

Thank you for always being there
And loving me like you do.
So much of who I am today,
Dear Grandmother, comes from you!

A Gift for You, Gramma

Here is a little gift,
Which I made just for you.
It is to cheer you
When nothing else can do.
Open up the lid and you will see:
It's full of hugs and kisses
Just for you from me!

Who Needs Santa when You Have Grandma!?

Mom's Christmas Without Dad

Mom, I know Christmas may be hard this year
Because of the loss of the wonderful love you had
With the loved one you called *husband*
And the dear one I called *Dad*.

I know that it is hard for you
To celebrate a special holiday
Without your sweetheart beside you
Since he was called away.

But know that he is with us
In everything we do,
For he lives inside of my heart
And in the heart of you.

So many times I see his face
In the eyesight of my heart
And know that of my very being
He has a noble part.

So celebrate Jesus's birth with me today,
And I will celebrate with you.
And we will thank the Lord above,
As we remember the joy Dad was to you.

And we will let this holiday
Be the best Christmas it can be,
For I hope that you see
A bit of Dad in me.

Every Heart Comes Home for the Holidays

My Dear Daughter

This is just a little note to say
Just how much I love you
On this special Christmas Day.

I hope that you know it
And have known it through the years,
As I kissed away your boo-boos
And dried your childhood tears.

I hope that you heard it
In every word I said,
Whether it was to say "Good morning"
Or that it was time for bed.

I hope that you felt my love
In every single embrace
And recognized it in the look
That you saw on my happy face.

I'm overwhelmed by the miracle
Of each and every day
That we have our lovely daughter
That God so lovingly sent our way!

So today I celebrate with vigor
And something special I wanted to do,
As today I put into a little verse
Just how much your mom loves you!

Sent with Love

You are Loved

The Christmas season
Has a special reason:
It reminds us of God's love,
That he would send His Son to earth
In a simple stable birth.

This time causes us to reflect
On those who are so dear
And tell them of the love in our hearts
That we feel for them all year!

This card is to tell you
That you mean so much to me,
And I hope that in my actions
This love you could always see.

But in case you didn't know it,
I'm setting the record straight:
I love you very much, dear friend,
And your life I celebrate!

Our Family

Our family, through the years,
Has had its share of laughter and of tears.
But whatever we do and whatever the weather,
We will come through the storms of life
TOGETHER!

The Spirit of Christmas is All Around Us

Son's Make Christmas Special

A wonderful blessing we have found,
Who to this special holiday
Adds so much happiness and joy,
Goes by the title of "our son" or "our boy".

With his energy and spirit
And his fun loving boyish way,
He keeps the family entertained
As they gather for the day.

I'm so glad when we get together
And all is said and done
That at our Christmas table
Sits our wonderful son.

Christmas With Our Sons

When all is said and done
Christmas is more special
Now that we have our sons!

Look! It's Christmas!

Look, everyone!
The date circled in red
Is finally here.
And today we celebrate
With Christmas cheer!
Let's take some photos
To record this day,
So the memory
Will never fade away!

Share the Spirit

Family Quilt

Our family is a like an heirloom quilt
With each piece of fabric a special part
Of our family's history
And of each other's heart.

Some of us are calicos,
Bright and colorful and fun.
Others may be more like silk,
Striving always to be number one.

Just like a quilt needs a design
And colors (soft as well as bold),
Our family quilt has need for both,
If our story is to be told.

All kinds of pieces are sewn in,
With stitches large and small.
And, in our family quilt of love,
We need them one and all!

We wish for you this Christmas
A season of peace and love
And the blessings of the One Who created
The family quilt we love!

Sometimes I Just Know
I'm the Fun-Loving Calico,
While Other Times I Feel like Silk So Fine,
Rather like a Vintage Wine.

A Christmas Wish for Our Lovely Daughter-in-Love

There is no card special enough for you.
So this little card will have to do,
Although it can only convey in part
The depth of love within our hearts.

You are our daughter,
The wife of our son.
And we are so blessed
That he chose such a wonderful one!

Although we didn't give birth to you
Or childhood illnesses nurse you through,
There is a special, wonderful bond we share.
For you are the answer to a lifelong prayer.

You are the special gift that God sent from above
To complete our family's circle of love.
He has blessed us so much with the gift of you ~~
Not only this Christmas, but our whole lives through!

So Merry Christmas, dear, lovely daughter-in-law.
But our daughter-in-love is who you are.
This little card is just a token
Of millions of loving wishes, too numerous to be spoken!

As Far as Daughters-in-Law Go,
You are Top of the Line:
The Best Daughter-in-Love
That We Could Ever Find!

A gift so fine...
That Daugter-in-law of Mine

It's a Family Thing

All the family is excited,
From the kids to the older folks.
Mom is in the kitchen cooking,
And Dad is cracking jokes!

The kids are dancing to DVDs,
As they make out their list
Of the things they want from Santa,
Including something with a disc...

The mailbox is full of cards,
And the turkey was bought today.
It is official now
That Christmas is on the way!

Will You be Home for Christmas?

Daddy, will you be home for Christmas?
It won't be the same without you.
Every night I pray for you,
And all day I think about you.

I asked God to send you back,
All safe and sound to me,
And told Him what a lovely gift
For Christmas that would be!

Please Come Home for Christmas

CHRISTMAS in LOVE

Your First Christmas Together

If Christmas has always been wonderful
(A time cherished and special to see),
Sharing your first Christmas together
Will show you how lovely it can be.

Each bough of the tree becomes important.
Each light and each ornament so fine,
Reminds you of your love for each other,
As love and tenderness in your faces shine.

This is your first "married" Christmas.
And so lovely is the sweet memory
That I know you look forward to the coming years,
So you can see just how marvelous it will be!

Christmas Roses

Here are some roses
To tell you that I love you
And show you just how much.
For each time you look at them
Your heart I hope they touch
And speak as loudly as roses do,
Declaring with their beauty
My undying love for you.

Our Newlywed Bliss and First Christmas Kiss

For My Husband on Christmas

I feel that I must tell you
(Even though I hope you can see)
How much I love you, sweetheart,
And how dear you are to me...

You are the husband
That I always hoped I'd find.
You are my sweetheart always ~~
I'm so thankful that you are mine!

You are the reason for my being;
You are the ornaments on my Christmas tree.
I am blessed beyond all measure,
Having you share your love with me!

I celebrate with you today
And can only try to count the ways
Of how you bring happiness to my life
And joy to my days!

Christmas is more special
Because you are near me,
And I'm whispering, *I love you.*
Can you hear me?

Merry Christmas, Hubby!

You are the husband that, I believe with all my heart,
God wanted me to find.
And every day I thank Him for you ~~
Wonderful sweetheart of mine!

Don't Sit under the Mistletoe with Anyone Else but Me

EARLY CHRISTMAS

I Know it isn't Christmas

I know it isn't Christmas
To anyone but me.
But I marked it on my calendar,
So everyone could see
That I have the Christmas spirit
And have it all year long.
So giving you this Christmas gift
Really isn't wrong!
I wish you a happy day, today
And throughout the year to come,
And pray that all your dreams come true,
Each and every one.

Happy Early Christmas

Some say that Christmas comes
Only once a year,
And that is what makes it special
And helps to keep it dear.
But sometimes in the middle
Of summer or of fall
A little bit of Christmas
Is the most special time of all.

So here's a little present
To bring a bit of cheer
And share my Christmas Spirit
In the middle of the year.

May Christmas be Evergreen in Your Heart

C is for Christmas

Is It Christmas Yet?

I awoke early this morning
As happy as I could be,
For it certainly felt
As if were Christmas to me.

There was a chill in the air,
And the house had such a happy feeling.
There was a sense of happiness everywhere,
From the floor up to the ceiling.

So I knew that it must be Christmas
Because of joy that just abounded.
But one look at the calendar
Showed that fact to be unfounded.

But I didn't let that stop me.
I just went right along,
Writing out my Christmas wishes
And singing Christmas songs.

I found this little gift
That reminded me of you.
So I'm sending it your way,
So you will enjoy my Christmas too!

December the first
Is finally here.
May we put up the tree?
I think the time is right,
But Mom may not agree!

Almost Christmas

LATE CHRISTMAS

Dreaming of a Late Christmas

Christmas is almost here.
And my confession is, I fear,
That (though I strive to do things right)
I'm so behind tonight!!

The house is a mess, I must confess,
And there is laundry in the hamper,
But I won't let it be a damper.
Not a single cookie, pie, or cake
Have I had the time to bake!

No tree awaits in my living room...
No lights outside to distill the gloom...
And not a single present, bought and wrapped so bright,
Hides in my closet on this night!!

But I will not despair or fret;
I just haven't started yet!
When the rest of you have had all your fun...
I'll think of mine as JUST BEGUN!!

When you are finished, I'll have the joy
Of shopping for some girl or boy
And baking some delightful cake.
Oh, what a memory that will make!!

I will not fret about it anymore.
I'll just run down to the scrapbook store
And get more film and paper and glue,
So I can scrap a page or two!

Christmas Mess and Truly Blessed

The Card I Meant to Send

Last Christmas I resolved
To start my cards right then,
When I would have time to ponder
The cards that I would send.

The cards would be so lovely,
Beautiful beyond compare:
The lovely masterpieces I would send
To show my friends I care.

The colors would be lovely.
And the cards would be 3-D,
All created and hand designed:
Totally and uniquely me!

Imagine the shock I felt,
When the calendar on my PC
Said my time had already run out,
And it was December 23!

So dear friends, I beg of you,
Do not despair or grieve.
For in my heart I love you still,
But this is the card you will receive...
From me.

Love,

Thena

P.S. I'm starting on next year's cards on Jan. 1^(st)...
And they will be lovely!!

Christmas Craziness

CHRISTMAS SPIRIT

Hurry, Christmas!

"Hurry, Christmas!"
Some would say.
"We want to celebrate
On Christmas Day!"

While others hope,
And even pray,
That the holiday
Could have a delay.

But I, for one,
Don't mind at all
Celebrating Christmas
In summer or fall.

I know that the
Most important part
Is celebrating Christmas
Each day in my heart.

Christmas Spirit

I have the Christmas Spirit
And want to share with you,
So that you can have joy
And peace the whole year through.
I'm sending you a little gift
And hope that it will bless,
Put a smile upon your face,
And bring you happiness!

Keep the Wonder of Christmas in Your Heart

Christmas Wouldn't be Christmas Without...

Christmas songs and Christmas trees
And quality time with the family,
Candy canes and blinking lights,
Staying up late Christmas Eve night,
Reading the Christmas Story
And drawing names,
Trying to remember the rules
For last year's boxed board games,
Baking cookies for family and friends
And praying that snowflakes will fall
To make this the most perfect Christmas of all!!

Just Another Day...

Christmas could never be
Just another day to me.
No matter if I get old and gray,
I will celebrate Jesus's birth
Every single Christmas Day!

Come and celebrate with me.
And we will decorate the tree,
Sing carols together loud and clear,
And give thanks for another year!

No More Stress

I won't worry or stress anymore
Over the kind of gifts
I can buy at the store.
But I will try my very best
To see that those I love are blessed.

The Most Wonderful Day of the Year!

Moments to Treasure

Joyous laughter on holidays,
Choosing a Christmas tree,
Holding a tiny baby,
Rocking little ones on my knee...

Watching the Christmas parade
Or working on a float...
Going to relatives by airplane,
Car, train or boat...

Watching the children's Christmas play,
Hearing little ones sing,
Watching the snowfall:
Each one is a special thing!

Going to the special services
To hear the Christmas Story,
Listening to the choir sing
Of Christmas and its glory...

I'll treasure these moments
And set them apart.
For these are the Christmas memories
I'll store in my heart.

I'm Celebrating Christmas...

From the first day of December until the last.
And I won't stop wishing everyone a joyous Christmas
Until the blessed day is past.
I will rise in the morning and think of all the joy
That came from Heaven to earth
In the form of a tiny baby boy.
You can celebrate your holidays
And say "Greetings of the Season."
But when I wish you a "Blessed Christmas,"
I'm remembering that Jesus is the Reason.

Christmas and Its Glory

Christmas in My Heart

I made a resolution
To do the best I can do
To keep the Christmas spirit
For the whole year through.

I will appreciate my neighbors
(More than in the past)
And pray that my good intentions
Throughout the year will last.

I will smile at other drivers,
As I travel in my car,
And will always be ready
To buy a kid a candy bar.

If I see a crying baby
Traveling in a plane,
From frowning at the noise
I will always refrain.

Through my daily life
I will take opportunities to share,
To lift someone's spirit,
And remember them in prayer.

And when Christmas comes again,
I hope someone will say,
"Merry Christmas to someone
Who acts like it's Christmas every day!"

Lights

I look at the lights on the Christmas tree.
I see the outside lights all aglow.
Out in garden the wind is blowing,
And now it's beginning to snow.

The lights make the snow so pretty,
As they shine so beautifully bright,
Adding so much excitement
To our special Christmas night.

Making Christmas Last All Year

I Love Christmas

I love Christmas!
I love it so very much!
It has a special feeling
And a very special touch.
It causes folks to smile
And say a kind hello.
Christmas gives the whole month
A special kind of glow!

Winter

In the winter,
come rain or snow,
The world takes on
A special glow.
We don our winter coats
And sweaters
And pull out comforters
Filled with feathers.
We seem to be drawn
Closer by the differences
That come with winter weather,
As we feel the closeness
And the wonderful coziness
Of just being together.

Christmas adds to the appeal
Of winter
With a warmth of its own ~~
A warmth so real
That each of us feel
A beauty of spirit
And an old-fashioned charm
That fills us with joy,
That helps keep us warm.

In a Winter Wonderland

Christmas is Coming

Christmas is coming!!
I can feel it in my spirit.
The holiday is fast approaching.
If you listen, you can hear it!

Christmas music is playing.
And people are smiling,
As they instinctively hum along
To their favorite hymn or Christmas song.

Decorations are up in the mall.
(Of course, they have been since November,
But it seems much more official now,
Since it is finally December!)

"Christmas is coming,"
I'm so happy to say.
Soon it will be here.
Christmas is on its way!

The Christmas Rush

In the hustle and the bustle,
And the sprees of shopping too,
There is something so important
That I must not forget to do!

I know I put it on my list ~~
I wrote it in red ink,
But I've been so very busy
That I've scarcely had time to think!

Oh, now I remember what it was ~~
I'm so embarrassed, but now I've got it!
Christmas is about the birth of Christ,
And I almost forgot it!

The True Spirit of Christmas

I Heard Christmas!

"Mommy! I heard it!
I heard Christmas today!"
And then my little one
Went back out to play!

Hurry, Hurry, Christmas

Hurry, hurry, Christmas;
Please do not be late.
I have so much to look forward to
I don't think that I can wait!

I asked Santa for a doll
And a car for her to ride in,
Along with a boy doll, as well,
So she can sit beside him.

I asked him for a purse for Mom,
Something nice and spiffy.
I know that she would like it
If it got here in a jiffy!

And Daddy needs a new remote,
So he can watch his TV show.
For the other one has disappeared.
Where it went: we do not know!

So hurry, hurry, hurry;
Please do not be late.
I just love Christmas,
But just can't stand the wait!

Christmas is a "Waity" Matter

What a Wonderful Time of the Year!

Christmas is such a wonderful time of the year
To share with all of those far and near
Who fill our hearts with love and joy,
From oldest matriarch to youngest girl or boy!

Each family member has a special part,
A treasured spot in each member's heart
That bonds each precious one to another:
Father, son, daughter, or mother.

Grandparents are celebrated
As the jewels they are to us all.
And how wonderful to hug close
The wonderful relatives we love the most!

We love the family gathering,
As relatives come from far and wide:
From city condominium
To the farming country side.

The day starts off early
With the awaking of each little one
Who is giddy with anticipation,
Eagerly awaiting the holiday fun!

❧

Just a little note to say:
Have a wonderful Christmas Day!

Just What I Always Wanted

Here Comes Christmas!

Christmas is coming,
And I can't wait.
The children are praying
That it won't be late.
The parents are busy shopping,
And the grandparents are excited.
For, with visits from the grandkids,
They will surely be delighted!
The stores are decorated,
And the cards are in the mail.
Oh, the days of the calendar
Are moving slowly as a snail!
The little ones can hardly stand it.
They agonize with the wait,
As they collect the Christmas cards
From the postman at their gate.
The puppy dog can sense it,
And the cat is purring at my knee.
And the excitement of the coming holiday
Is a special treat for me!

What is It about Christmas?

What is it about Christmas
That makes so many people smile
And forget about their worries
For just a little while?

What is it about Christmas
That, to each girl and boy,
Says that they can share
In some special holiday joy?

What is it about Christmas
That makes it special in every way?
It is because we know
The Christ Child was born that day!

It's Beginning to Feel a Lot like Christmas

The Delight of Christmas Night

I love the thrill of Christmas
And the happiness it brings
To so many people on God's earth,
His special human beings!

I love the faces of the children,
Filmed in the candle's glow,
Their childish exuberance
And the excitement that they show.

I love the gradual buildup
And the frenzy at the mall.
I love the sounds of carols.
Oh, I really love it all!

I love wrapping packages
Of gifts to mail out,
The sending of cards to friends...
That's what it's all about!

I love the special Christmas services
And visiting with family and friends.
And I love Christmas night,
When comes the season's end!

❧

The calendar says the season has come to an end,
And soon a brand new year will begin!

Ah, the Sugar Plum Fairies!

Music Makes Christmas So Special

Music makes Christmas so special,
As the notes waft through the air ~~
From pianos and organs at church
To speakers at the mall and everywhere.

Music speaks to our spirit
And is felt by the heart and soul.
To be as beautiful inside as Christmas music
Is my holiday goal!

Service to Others

Washing the car,
Feeding the kitty,
Helping to clean,
Making things pretty,
Helping mom in the kitchen,
Or Dad in the yard...
Doing things for others
Isn't really hard.
Welcoming new neighbors,
Babysitting my brother,
Obeying God's Word,
And loving one another...
For Christmas this year
Will be only the start
Of the holiday spirit
I plan to keep in my heart.
Let's all celebrate
With each loving act we do ~~
But keep on celebrating
The whole year through.

Christmas Angels

Christmas

C ome and celebrate with us
H onor Jesus's birth
R ejoice with us
I n celebration here on earth
S ing Christmas carols
T ake time to appreciate
M any wonderful blessings
A s with friends and family you share
S pecial Christmas joy and a Christmas prayer.

Waiting...

The snow is falling.
The tree is decorated.
And friends and family are arriving,
For whom we have been waiting!

I know Christmas will come.
And I try not to worry,
But I just wish so much
That Christmas would hurry!

Away in a Manger

CHRISTMAS GIFTS

A Special Gift

Here's a special teddy bear
Who is looking for a home,
A little girl or boy
To call his very own.

He is a loyal teddy
And will be a trusting friend,
Who will turn a frowny face
Into a happy grin.

Don't tell him that Christmas
Is a little while away
Because he thinks
That Christmas is today.

I didn't have the heart
To make this special teddy wait
To come and live with you
And help you celebrate.

A Christmas Craft

I may look like a simple little dress,
But with dual duty I am blessed.
I can make your room
Smell nice and sweet
By holding a potpourri treat.
Or if you hang your clothes on a line,
Put your pins in this pocket of mine!

I Can "Bearly" Wait till Christmas

For My Dad at Christmas

Wonder what I ever did
To be such a fortunate kid.
I'm the happiest kid I know
To have a dad who loves me so!

I put my picture in this card
For you to carry each day,
To remind you how much I love you
When you are far away.

In this card is a special prayer
That all your dreams come true.
I can ask for no better gift
Than to have a dad like you!

Our Gift for Mom

Mommy, here's a coupon book
That I created for you
To give you the benefit
Of things I know how to do.
I will make my bed
And get to school on time.
And the good thing is
The coupons are free ~~
They won't cost you a dime!

A Gift for You

This little gift is just for you
To let you know I care.
And on this special day
It's sent your way
With a special Christmas prayer.

Santa's Little Helper

A Little Gift

This little stuffed toy
Needs a new home,
A sweet cuddly kid
Of his very own.

I know it isn't Christmas
And won't be for awhile.
But if you could pretend it is,
It would make Teddy smile.

So sing Jingle Bells
And get in the Christmas spirit,
For you never know
Just who may need to hear it.

Because You are Special

This is an early present
That I have chosen to send
In honor of Christmas
And because you are my friend.

Sometimes, due to things that happen,
We cannot gather as we would choose.
So celebrating when we can
Helps to keep away the blues.

So Merry Christmas, Dearest Friend.
I hope you enjoy your little gift,
That it brightens up your day
And gives your heart a lift!

Santa was Here

Rudolph BOO!

So you found a reindeer
Hanging on your door?
And now you're wondering
Just what it's for!
It means that Rudolph
Has gone out of his way
To wish you a wonderful and blessed
Christmas holiday!
You must now pass him on,
As you walk down the street,
To some neighborhood friends
Or some that you'd like to meet!

Santa BOO!

So you found ole Santa
Hanging on your door?
And now you're wondering
Just what he's there for!
It means that Santa Claus
Has gone out of his way
To wish you a wonderful and blessed
Christmas holiday!
Even though he's busy
And in charge of lots of elves,
He took the time to remind us
To think of others, not just ourselves!
You must now pass him on,
As you walk down the street,
To some neighborhood friends
Or some that you'd like to meet!

Then One Foggy Christmas Eve...

Christmas BOO!

Rudolph has a red nose
To help guide Santa's sleigh
And show the other aircraft
That it has the right of way.
He is a wee bit nosey
And wants to see what others do
To prepare their homes for Christmas,
So he came to visit you!
Just enjoy the Christmas spirit,
When you find him on your door,
And then pass him on to someone else.
That's what he is for!
He wants you to pass on to your neighbors
The fun and Christmas cheer
That can only come by sharing
The joy of Christmas this year!

BOO to You!

This is a fun tradition
Of making something cute
(Like a little Rudolph
Or Santa in his suit)
And hanging it on a neighbor's door ~~
Only to run away,
So that they won't know it was you
Who wished them a happy day.

Christmas Surprises

Christmas Gifts

Johnny got inline skates for Christmas
And a new laptop PC.
But he is a lot bigger
And much older than me.
Sue Sue is the baby,
So she got twin dolls in a bed.
One of them cries real tears
When it needs to be fed.
I'm waiting here impatiently
For Dad my name to call ~~
HEY! I got an iPOD!
It's the best gift of them all!

Look at the gifts
Under the tree.
Some are for you,
And some are for me.
I think it's more fun
(And I get so excited)
To see others open my gifts
And be surprised and delighted!

Look at all the packages
Underneath the tree.
I know that lots of them
Are especially for me!
Each one of them
Was chosen with such care,
Wrapped with loving hands,
Which carefully placed them there!

O Christmas Tree

Apples for the Teacher

They set them on my desk.
They set them on my chair.
I can hardly walk around the room,
For there are apples every where.

It isn't that I don't like apples.
I think they're good to eat,
Especially juicy red ones
That taste so crisp and sweet.

I have stuffed ones made of velvet,
Ceramic ones so fine,
Decanter apples (if you can imagine)
Filled with a tiny bit of wine.

I have bright red plastic ones
And wooden ones so spiffy.
You tell me the type you want,
I can find one in a jiffy.

Each one carried by tiny hands
And lovingly brought to me:
That's why I can't bear to part
With a single one, you see!

But after 20 years of teaching,
Of apples I have had my share.
So, perhaps, next year at Christmas
Someone will send me a... pear?

The Present Pile

Handprint Poems

I left my little handprint,
So that you will always see
That this ornament was made
By someone who loves you... ME!

I will grow up,
And my handprint will change.
But the love that made this
Will always remain.

Merry Christmas, Mom and Dad!
I want to do my part,
So I'm leaving you my handprint.
(You already have my heart.)

To show you the love that's in my heart
I left my little handprint here,
To remind you at Christmas time
Of the love I feel throughout the year!

Look at this little print
That I made for you.
You can put it in your book
To remember the Christmas I was two!

This Little Light of Mine...

CHRISTMAS FAITH

Christmas is Special

Christmas time is special.
And all the world seems blessed
With love and kindness
And seems at its gentlest.
We seem more aware of others
And the needs that they have too.
Our hearts search for kindnesses
And loving things to do.
But as we worship together,
Let us resolve to do our part
To celebrate Christmas all year long,
By keeping it in our hearts!

Angels Watching over Us

Angels are watching over us
And guarding our little home.
For God has blessed us bountifully
And His love has daily shown.

We feel it in the routine
Of our lives each day.
We feel blessed to be together,
Whether working or at play.

At Christmas time,
We all agree:
Home for the holidays
Is the place we want to be.

The Real Meaning of Christmas

What I Got for Christmas

The best gift I got for Christmas
Was over 2000 years ago.
There were no parades or banners
And no new fallen snow.

The angels sweetly sang,
And shepherds rushed to see
Just exactly what the star
Shinning in the east might be.

Wisemen knew it was their King,
Born on this holy day.
And the best gift I ever got
Was from many miles and years away.

But it was a gift for me
And a gift for you as well,
A gift that fills my heart with joy
And gives me a wonderful story to tell.

Wish I Could Have been There

I wish I could have been there
On that first Christmas Day
To hear the angels singing
And see where the Baby lay.

I wish I could have been there
To see Joseph and Mary in the stable
And sense the hush of the animals
As they peered toward the cradle.

What a great thing to see the kings
(The wisemen) and shepherds come
To bring their gifts in reverence
To the newborn Holy One.

Wisemen Still Seek Him

Christmas Service

I love to go to Christmas Services
And love to hear the special songs.
I love the Christmas carols,
And I always sing along.
I love the Children's Program,
And each year I long to be
One of the special wisemen.
But they only ask for three.
Maybe I will be a shepherd
When the time comes around next year.
But this year I'm in the chorus,
And I'm singing loud and clear!

Sunday Best

On Christmas Day our family's blest,
And we put on our Sunday best
To go to church and celebrate the day
That God sent a special babe this way.
When we come home, we have a meal.
And the love we show is very real,
As we gather together with each other:
Brother, sister, father and mother.
We bow our heads and say a prayer,
Feeling God's presence everywhere:
From the church service to the family meal,
As God's immense love each of us feel.

The Stars in the Sky Looked Down Where He Lay...

Home to Heaven for Christmas

"I'll be home for Christmas," she said
And then turned out the light.
Angels came and took Mom home ~~
Home for Christmas on that night.

Mom went home for Christmas;
She knew it all along.
"I'll be home for Christmas,"
She sang it like a song...

Mom went home for Christmas.
She smiled and left us there.
We knew it was her heart's desire;
We knew it was her prayer.

Mom went home for Christmas.
And though we miss her here,
I know that she is happy now,
And I feel that she is near.

Mom went home for Christmas.
I know that she couldn't wait.
And I know that she'll welcome me someday,
When I get to Heaven's gate.

What a Wonderful Christmas Mom Will Have.
What a Wonderful Christmas Day It Will be,
To be There to Celebrate Jesus's Birth
And His Wonderful Face to See!

Come Together at Christmas

Let us celebrate together,
As our gifts we bring,
The joy of knowing Jesus ~~
The Baby who was King.
He did not stay in the cradle,
And we should not try to keep Him there,
But should celebrate His birth,
As our blessings with others we share.
Let us each resolve to honor Him
In a very special way,
By doing acts of love and kindness
To celebrate His birthday!

I Will Celebrate

I will celebrate Your birth,
And I will share Your love today,
By doing things to show my love
In a very special way.

I know I'm just one person,
And I can't change the world,
But goodness can begin with
One single boy or girl.

So I'm out to change my world
By doing what I can
And saying, "Happy Birthday, Jesus;
Let me be Your helping hand!"

Christ Completes Christmas

The Joy of Believing in Christmas

There is a special joy in believing
In the Virgin Birth,
A joy in the celebration
Of a savior sent to earth.

There is a joy that fills my heart
And seems to overflow.
I am so happy that I believe in Him
And want everyone to know!

There's joy in the Christmas Story
And joy in each song,
Bringing peace to each believer
Who loves to sing along!

I'm Glad I Believe in Christmas

I love the way I feel at Christmas.
I love the special sights.
I love the brush of angels' wings
And the glint of Christmas lights.
I'm so glad I believe in Christmas
And the Baby sent to earth,
So glad that I celebrate Christmas
As our blessed Savior's birth!

Jesus is the Reason for the Season

PETS

Christmas is Purr-fection

Christmas is purr-fection.
It just cannot be beat.
My stocking is filled to the brim
With the very "micest" treats!

My humans really love me;
They are the cat's meow.
They treat me so specially,
Like I'm their favorite pal!

I feel bad for the other cats,
Who do not live with me,
For my Christmas was just purr-fect.
I'm as contented as can be!!

Merry Christmas from Your Doggie

Bow wow wow.
Ruff ruff ruff.
Wooooof woooof woof.

Translation:
May your Christmas be great
In every single way.
And may you have a joyful
And wonderful holiday!

Meowy Christmas!

Merry Christmas to My Doggie

Merry Christmas, little doggie friend,
On this wonderful holiday.
Did you know that animals were in the stable
Where tiny Baby Jesus lay?

I wonder if they knew what was happening
And why people were so elated,
Bringing gifts to the little Babe,
Whose birth they celebrated.

Such thoughts make me look at you
In a very different way,
Thankful that I have my pet
To share this special day.

Merry Christmas, Kitty Cat

Merry Christmas to my kitty.
My *purr-fectly* wonderful pal,
Who stays close beside me
And is my sweet, furry gal.

I love you, little kitty,
And I hope you understand
These words I say,
When I tell you in English:
Happy Christmas Day!

Not a Creature was Stirring, Not Even a Mouse

Doggie Christmas

It's Christmas time,
And the house is busy.
People are running around ~~
Things are in a tizzy.

But here I sit,
Like a bump on a log;
Everyone forgets
To buy gifts for the dog!

Wait! I smell something
Underneath the tree!
It's in a rawhide package,
So it must be for me!

Oh joy! I'm as happy
As happy can be
That on Christmas
The family thought of me!

A "Tail" of Woe

My tail is down
And is not waggin'.
My heart is heavy,
And my spirit, saggin'.
The family went off
With a Christmas tree,
Which means they're celebrating
Without inviting me!

Remember to "Paws" for Christmas

CHRISTMAS PLACES

Christmas in the Tropics

Christmas in the Tropics
Is a very special sight.
Although no snow falls on Christmas Eve,
It's still an awe filled night.

The weather can be sweet and balmy,
And palm trees may gently sway,
But still the message is the same
That we hear on Christmas Day.

I love Christmas in the cold northeast,
Where snowflakes always seem to fall.
But my Christmas in the Tropics ~~
I love the best of all!

For I was with you in the warmth
Of a special tropical holiday,
And sweet memories of that time
Will never ever go away.

A California Christmas

It's Christmas in California,
Where Santa dresses in shorts.
And people are out on the beach,
Playing all types of sports.
But the spirit of the holiday
Is the same here in the west
As it is in the snowy east.
It's just that our weather's best!

I'm Dreaming of a Green Christmas!

Country Christmas

A little secret I must confess:
A country Christmas is the best,
Filled with wonderful holiday fun
That makes the day for everyone.
We plan the day for months before;
It is the day we wait all year for.
And, when it comes, we all agree
That it is the best day there could be!

Kinfolks come from miles around,
Leaving the city and getting out of towns.
They knock at our door with smiling faces,
And get lost in the huddles and cuddles and embraces.
We've cleaned and cooked and wrapped all night,
So that we can be up before it's light
And snuggle in PJs and robes and such,
As the gifts we open and share and touch.

The breakfast will be hot and served with laughter.
Then we will start preparations right after
For the biggest dinner that you could think up,
With treats for everyone right down to the pup!

Oh, I pity the city folks who live in town,
Whose Christmas starts off with a traffic frown.
They must buy a turkey all frozen and stiff
And shop at the mall for a Christmas gift.
I pity the folks with the artificial tree,
When the whole green woods is there for me!

I love the gift making and the homemade fun
That make the day special for everyone.
Yes, I love my Christmas. I must admit:
For me a Country Christmas is the very best fit!!

Homespun Holidays are Stitched with Love

SANTA is REAL

Scrapper's Wish List

Santa, I've been awful good this year,
And I deserve a break!
I need some brand new albums
For all the photos that I take.

I make the beds most every day.
(Or at least I do sometimes,
If I'm not scrapbooking
Or checking in with my buddies online...)

I cook dinner and wash the dishes
And fold the laundry neatly.
(And when I start a roll of film,
I finish it completely!)

I walk the dogs and feed the cats
And buy shavings for the hamster.
(And never once did I download
A single file from Nampster!)

I vacuum the floors
And mop the kitchen.
And I dust... most every day.
(Well, at least often enough
To keep the Health Dept. away!)

So here's my list of things I need,
Some things that I desire.
And when you come on Christmas Eve,
There will be cookies near the fire!

Dear Santa, How Good Do I Have to be?

Dear Good Little Girls and Boys,

I'm sending off this letter
Just to let you know
That everything is right on time,
And there is plenty of snow.
The elves have been so busy,
Making toys right and left,
So that there is barely room
To place them on a shelf!
Rudolph has his nose shined
To a highly polished glow,
So that, in the dark of night,
I can see just where to go!
Mrs. Claus has shinned my boots
And ironed my suit of red,
Although you won't see it,
For you will be sleeping in your bed!
I read all of your letters
And know exactly where you are,
So don't forget the milk and cookies ~~
Please leave them by the fire.
Santa

I have a dog.
I have a cat.
For Christmas, dear Santa,
Please bring me a rat!
A nice, white rat
In a sturdy cage
Is what I'd really enjoy.
I guess the desire
For owning one
Is built into a boy!

Dear Santa, I Want One of Everything!

Santa and Me

Santa comes to visit
On the night of Christmas Eve,
But you have to ask him earlier
For the gifts you will receive.

I am really new at this.
You see, I am quite small,
So it strikes me as very strange
That you tell Santa at the mall!

I huggled up in Santa's lap,
But I don't know if he heard
The list I had to tell him,
Since I can't speak a word!

Perhaps when I am older,
I can tell him like I should.
But until I learn to speak,
I'll just concentrate on being good!

Santa Because

I know who he is.
I can tell by the beard on his chin
And by his big belly
And his big ole grin.

That he is Santa
Is plain to see.
I just hope he remembers
On Christmas Eve
That I am ME!

Cutest Little Elf

Santa's Wonderland

Way up North is a place, they say,
That Santa and his reindeer stay.
It is a very happy land
That is fun, unique and very grand.

They say that Santa has a shop
Where, all year long, work never stops.
And toys of all kinds line its shelves,
All handmade by little elves.

They say the snow falls all year long,
And happy folks sing Christmas songs
And whistle merrily as they go ~~
At least, they tell me this is so.

They say that reindeer fly and paw,
The most beautiful that you ever saw,
With one whose nose is brightest red
To guide the way for Santa's sled.

They say the place is always the same
And say that Santa knows your name
And that this is his home each day,
As he waits for Christmas to come your way.

They say that's where Santa's sleigh
Is polished and oiled
And shined up so bright
To get it ready for Christmas Eve night.

Well, I can't say for sure that this is so,
But it was told to me by someone
Who should know...

Santa Claus is Coming to Town

First Visit with Santa

I met Santa
And sat on his lap.
He had a soft belly,
A nice place for a nap!

I liked his white beard
And the jolly look on his face.
His arm encircled me,
Like a grandfatherly embrace.

I liked Santa just fine,
And I think he liked me,
But my Mommy's and Daddy's arms
Are still the best place to be!

Photo with Santa

Look at this cute little photo,
And what a precious grin!
I love the way your outfit looks,
And, my, you're looking thin!

It looks as if you are enjoying
This fun experience at the mall.
And I must say,
Without further delay,
You are the cutest Santa of all!

Santa and Me

Santa Claus

Please come to visit.
Don't forget me, please.
We don't have a chimney,
So Mom sent you our keys!

After you put the presents
Underneath the Christmas tree,
Just pull the door closed behind you
And on the table please leave our key.

Dear Santa,

Hanging on our door
Is a very special key.
Mom says that it is magic
And only you can see!

Please use that key
When you come to visit me,
For we are a modern family
With no fireplace or chimney!

Dear Kids,

Please don't worry about ole Santa,
If you don't have a chimney for me.
I can use your front door to visit you,
For I have a magic key!

Christmas is a "Claus" for Celebration

Santa, Mommy and Me

I think that Mommy talks to Santa,
For I wrote to him and said
That I had been a real good kid,
Cleaned my room and made my bed.

The bad times, I wrote him,
Were things far beyond my control.
But when I reached in my Christmas stocking,
I still found a lump of coal!

Mommy says that Santa comes at night
And quietly down our chimney climbs.
That dusty chimney must be such a tight squeeze.
That would explain why, just last year,
I thought I heard Santa sneeze!

We wanted a puppy for Christmas,
One to cuddle, train and pet.
But from the looks of the new nursery,
That is not what we're going to get!

If Santa's elves are so very wise,
And his workshop is so good,
Why don't they create a self-powered sleigh?
I really think they should!

Naughty or Nice... I've Made the List Twice

Oh No!

My friends said there was no Santa,
And it scared me for a bit.
But then I saw our tree was up
And, oh, so brightly lit.
I put the cookies on the table
And left Santa Claus a note.
The next day I had a reply,
And this is a quote:
"Thank you for the cookies
And the chocolate bar.
I've always been impressed
By what a smart kid you are!"
So, I suppose they were wrong
And not really very wise.
I imagine on Christmas morning
They will have a nice surprise!

Dear Santa,

Each Christmas Eve we put a key
Right outside our door,
Then we sweetly go to sleep,
Worrying no more.

No one else can use the key,
Not even you or me.
It only works for Santa Claus.
It's magic, don't you see?

Christmas is a Time to Believe in Things You Can't See

Santa is Scary...

There's a round little ole man,
Wearing a funny red suit,
Sitting in a fancy chair.
He comes to the mall once a year,
And the kids all meet him there!

He calls the kids one by one
To come and sit on his lap.
Well, Mommy said that
It was my turn,
But I really just wanted to nap!

They had me sit on the jolly man's lap,
And his beard looked fake to me!
I thought to myself, as I spied his elf,
"What could the purpose of all this be?"

I really tried so hard to be polite
And not let him know of my fear.
But before you could say "boo"
(Or "How do you do?"),
My face was creating a tear!!

Mommy and Daddy,
I really tried.
But Santa is scary,
And I cried and cried!

Maybe someday he and I could be friends,
And I won't be afraid of him then.
But for now I'd rather stay at home
And order my gifts on eBay or the telephone!!

On Santa's Knee

CHRISTMAS PRAYERS

A Christmas Prayer for You

Sometimes our lives bring things
That we don't understand,
And it is difficult to see
Just where was the Master's Hand.

But God will work all things out,
If we just give Him the chance to do
The things He knows are the best,
And then He will see us through.

So my Christmas prayer for you
Is that God above would bless
Your life, your day, your very being,
With peace, joy, love and happiness!

A Christmas Prayer

Lord, please create a cradle in my heart,
Where Baby Jesus can be born,
And let the love within me
Be enough to keep Him warm...

And, Father, let Your love flow through me
In such a special way
That the wonderful joy of Christmas
Would stay with me every day!

Oh, make my heart a worthy place
For the Child to come and stay.
And I thank You for that greatest gift
You gave us on Christmas Day!

Have a Blessed Christmas

Prayer for Friends

Father in Heaven up above,
I know that You love the ones we love
And know the pain they're going through
And how helpless we feel as to what to do!

For Christmas I would ask You to bless
Each of my friends here with happiness ~~
With love and laughter that will never cease,
But will each day only increase!

And, Father, for those hurting ones I seek
Complete healing for each friend so sweet.
I ask that You would bless and heal each one today
And send joy upon joy along their way!

For those whose houses are needing repair,
I know that You can send workmen there
And touch bosses' hearts that need to be touched
And provide funds when times are tough.

For those who have been feeling ill,
I ask in accordance with Your will
That You would heal their illness too,
And all the thanks we'll give to You!

For those whose spirits need a touch,
Who are feeling rather down today,
We ask a touch from Your dear hand
To chase all despair and gloom away!

For those whose marriages might need
Your loving hand to intercede,
This touch I ask for each and every one:
Let their love be renewed, loving and fun!

For those whose finances need healing,
I pray that You would help them too
And provide the funds to see them through.

And for those with cares unspoken,
Who are near despair,
With hearts so broken...
We lift those friends up to You
And ask You to touch them through and through!

And for each of those with children here,
We ask that You take away all fear
Of what the future might now hold
With terrorists on the rampage so bold!

Father, we know that the safest place on earth ~~
Without You there ~~ would be the worst.
But where You are and in Your embrace
Becomes the world's safest place!

So please keep us each one in Your care,
And let us know that You are there.
No matter what the world may do,
Keep us hugged safe, close to You!

In Jesus's Name,
Amen

God Answers Prayers at Christmas
And the Whole Year Through —
Every day Throughout the Year,
Dear Friend, I Pray for You.

THANK-YOUS

A Thank-You Gift for You

I'm so glad that you are you
And do the things that only you do!
You make me so very glad, you see,
And make me happy to be me.

I like myself when I'm with you
And doing things we like to do.
And throughout the years, it would seem,
That you and I are quite a team!

Thank You to _____

Just a little something to say
That I'm thinking of you today.
I hope your Christmas season is blessed
With joy and peace and happiness!

One More Time

I'm sending you this note at Christmas
To thank you one more time
For all the thoughtful things you do
And for being a friend of mine!

Honorary Elf

Merry Christmas to Our Sitter

What do you say to an angel sent to earth
Who has loved and nurtured your kids?
What do you do to show your appreciation
For the wonderful things she did?
Well, the angel lady is you,
And we are sending this card to say
How wonderful we think you are
And send our love your way!

For a Wonderful Sitter

For years you've nurtured our kids,
And you touched the hearts of those you've met.
This little card is to show you
That those who love you don't forget.
Our prayer is that it blesses you,
As you look at the names inside.
And know that when we say "our sitter/our friend,"
We say it with love and pride.

Merry Christmas !

✎

Thank you for the Christmas gift.
It's nice as it can be.
How great it is to have someone
Who is so nice to me!

You Make Christmas Brighter

Thank You, Soldier

May God bless you, dear soldier,
For all you do for us each day.
We will keep you in our hearts,
And for your safety we will pray.
We know that you have left your home and family,
As you answer your country's call.
You have made an awesome sacrifice,
And you are a hero to us all.
You will be missed so much at Christmas ~~
It will not be the same without you.
Our hearts are filled to the brim with love,
As we pray for you and think about you.
Our prayers are always with you.
And in our hearts we hug you tight,
Asking God to bless you on this Christmas:
Morning, noon and night!

Mail Carrier (or Newspapers, etc.)

Just a little note to say:
You're someone special in my day.
You take your task so seriously
To bring letters and parcels
Directly to me.

I know that you consider it to be
Just part of your job, and I agree
That it is your job, but only in part.
The rest of it comes from the love in your heart.

Here's a little gift to thank you
For the daily diligence that I see.
I hope that it will make you smile
And know that you have blessed me.

Wonder, Beauty and Awe of Christmas

Merry Christmas and Thank You

Just a little note from my heart to say:
Thank you my special friends on Christmas Day!
Thank you for the way you care
And for the compassion,
Which with me you share.

During this time so difficult to get through,
Each time I see your loving faces,
I'm thankful that God sent you
To encourage and inspire me
With the warmth of your embraces.

If ahead of me dark days
And painful times should abound...
Through it all I will be so grateful
For the wonderful, faithful friends,
Which, in you, I have found.

Thank You to Our Vet

It's Christmas time,
And we can't forget
To wish a Merry Christmas
To our favorite vet!

You treat our pets,
Who are so special and sweet.
And as a thank-you we're sending
This little holiday treat!

An Elf's Work is Never Done

A Blessed Christmas for Pastor and His Wife

We wanted to send you a special card
On this Christmas Day
To wish you season's greetings
And send our thanks your way.
But we faced such a dilemma
That it was difficult to do.
For how does one say thanks
To someone as wonderful as you?

How do we say "thank you" to people such as you,
Who take the time to help others,
Each day the whole year through?
How can we express our appreciation
And gratitude in such a way
That you will understand how heartfelt
Are the words that we will say?
How do we express the love we have for you
And how your faithfulness inspires us all,
With the way you hear and respond in obedience,
When you hear God's voice call?

How do we let you know that we are aware
Of the time you spend with your church family
In visits, counseling, fellowship and prayer ~~
Never really thinking of yourself at all,
But thinking first and foremost of others,
Who you think of as family:
Your sisters and your brothers?

There are no words adequate
For what we would love to do.
But for starters let us just say:
Merry Christmas! We love you!

Guided by the Light of Love

Merry Christmas to Our Church Secretary

We don't always take the time
To adequately express to you
Our heartfelt appreciation
For all the wonderful things you do.
But at Christmas time, this seems to be
The absolutely perfect and ordained opportunity!
Thank you for so many things
That you do each day,
From the smallest task that one would ask
To the biggies that come your way.
You handle each one with such finesse
And work with grace under fire.
Consider this little Christmas card a note of thanks
For the wonderful person you are!

Preaching to the Choir

We tease about how, sometimes,
We are preaching to the choir.
But, folks, it is no joke,
When I say how wonderful you are!
Your voices blend so wonderfully,
As your songs you send our way.
And never do you sound as lovely
As you do on Christmas Day!
We appreciate so very much
The contribution from each of you
To fill our hearts and souls with beauty
By the music that you do.

Holy, Happy Holidays

Sunday School Teacher

Christmas time would not be complete
Without a special card for you
To thank you for teaching our class
In a way that is uniquely you!

It is my prayer that this card would give you
At least a hint of how we feel,
Those of us you teach,
And it would our hearts reveal.

We daily thank God
For the person that is you
And are so grateful for
The loving things you do!

Christmas is the time
To thank our pastor
(We should have done it faster),
To applaud our choir
(How grateful we are!),
To thank our secretaries,
our organist,
our custodian,
our librarians,
our teachers,
For they are our "reach-ers."

You're on My "Nice List"

Merry Christmas to Our Pediatrician

For years you have given to others
And lost sweet time with family and wife,
Putting other people first
And putting off some areas of your life.

You are always ready to help us,
When we need your expertise.
And you do your best to calm our fears
And put our minds at ease.

You know that our children
Are our source of concern and joy.
And you treat with such tenderness
Every little girl and boy!

We have watched you in various situations,
As you have so patiently and lovingly tended
To each of your little patients
With the gentleness that God intended.

So it is with hearts full of gratitude
That we send this Christmas card to you.
And because of your wonderful, giving spirit,
We pray that God's blessings will rain down on you.

Have a wonderful holiday!

I Made the "Nice List"

Happy Holidays to Our Band Director

We owe our thanks to you
For the music we hear everywhere
And in everything we do:
It would not have been that way,
If it weren't for you.

You taught us more than band.
You let us hear what words can't tell.
You led us into a love affair with music
And let us feel its powerful spell.

"Merry Christmas!" is a wish
That comes straight from my heart,
With such gratitude for all you do,
As you share with us your art.

Christmas Bouquet

Thank you for thinking of us
On this special holiday
By sending us your loving thoughts
And a simply beautiful bouquet!
It meant so very much to us,
And its fragrance filled our place.
And love for you fills our hearts,
Just as those flowers filled the vase!

The Sounds of Christmas

A Christmas Wish for Someone Special

There is no card special enough for you.
So this little card will have to do,
Although it can only convey in part
The depth of love within our hearts.

You are the special gift that God sent from above
To complete our family's circle of love.
He has blessed us so much with the gift of you ~~
Not only this Christmas, but the whole year through.

You've been there for us,
Through thick and thin,
And blessed our lives,
Time and again.

As a Christmas blessing,
This little card is just a token
Of millions of loving wishes
Too numerous to be spoken!

A Little Note

Just a little Christmas note
Sent to you today
To tell you that I'm thankful
That God sent you my way!

Glad Tidings We Bring!

TRADITIONS

Everyone Needs a Tradition

Everyone needs a tradition,
And tradition needs a place to start.
And though some involve material things,
Each tradition starts in one's heart.

A little birthday plate can be used as such,
A place from which a tradition can grow:
The tradition of presenting special cakes on it.
And in time your family heritage will show.

The taking of a family photo,
Decorating of the family Christmas tree,
Reading of a favorite story
At every opportunity....

Bath time fun with the kids
That involves splashing and giggling out loud,
Dancing to the newest CD
Or celebrating special events with a crowd...

Gathering the family together for devotions,
Shopping together for Mother's Day at the mall,
Bringing everyone home for birthdays
And together giving far away relatives a call...

Traditions can be very simple;
They don't have to involve major plans.
A tradition can be as simple
As, at family meal time prayers, holding hands.

Treat each tradition gently throughout the years.
And down through the ages it will be
Treasured and cherished and loved
As part of your history.

Holiday Happenings

Christmas Jammies

Christmas is coming,
And Santa is on his way.
I can hardly wait
Until it's Christmas Day.

Mommy gave us jammies
And slippers for our feet.
And we will be all cozy,
As we await our Christmas treat!

Do you think that Santa notices
That we look spiffy as we sleep,
As we wear our matching Christmas jammies,
While we count our Christmas sheep?

I really love the jammies
That Mommy gave us today;
They make it much more fun
To wait for Christmas Day!

Put on your Christmas PJs
And jump into your snuggly bed.
Cuddle with your teddy bear
And pull the covers over your head.

Tonight is a very special night,
One we've watched for all year long.
And we know for sure tonight's the night,
For we have our Christmas jammies on!

Kids are Coming

The kids are coming for Christmas,
Even the dog is excited.
It's been a while since we've seen them,
And we are quite delighted.

The kids are coming for Christmas.
I do hope they won't be late.
They are grown up and on their own:
One kid is 64, and one kid is 68!

Twas the Night Before Christmas

Christmas PJs

Every year at Christmas,
We do a special thing:
We wear Christmas PJs
That Santa always brings!

It started when we were little.
And now our tradition has become...
We love our Christmas jammies
Just like when we were young!

The little ones get sleepers.
And the teens get stylish threads,
While Mom gets a nightie.
And Gramma gets flannel... red!

Dad and Grampy's favorites are traditional,
With piping on the yoke.
And sometimes Mom gets him Santa-silky ones,
But we know it is a joke!

We may have trends that come and go,
As our family changes and grows.
But come Christmas, it's pajama time,
And everybody knows!

Christmas Candles

I bought some Christmas candles
At the end of last December.
I put them away for
This Christmas Day,
But where... I can't remember!

Silent Night

Our Little Family

We don't have a large family.
There are just the three of us,
But when Christmas comes
We make the biggest fuss!

It is the celebration
That each one of us adores.
And we decorate our home
From the ceiling to the floors!

I do a bit of baking
(My special cookies are a must).
And not a single decoration
Is left in the attic to the dust!

We pull out all the ribbons,
(We shine the candle holders too),
While we hang up the stockings
(Mine happens to be blue).

The puppy dogs are startled
That their home has been transformed.
And they too get in the spirit
With new sweaters to keep them warm.

Thena's Christmas Fudge

I pride myself on giving treats
That don't come from the mall.
I like to give creative gifts
To all who come to call.
But this year the time slipped by,
And my mojo would not budge.
But in that fine Christmas tradition,
I'm still sending you my special Christmas fudge!

A Season of Love and Laughter

May Your Bulbs Beam Brightly

And the tree was all trimmed;
We'd had our eggnog
And sung our hymns...
So we turned on the switch
To light up the tree
And, with eyes fastened to it,
What did we see!?
Not one little light of the 300 or so
Was casting a twinkle
Or even a glow!!
We sat there in silence,
No one wanting to say
That there would be no lights
On this Christmas Day.
So we tested and tried,
Till we were blue in the face.
And not one little twinkle
Did our tree grace...
Then, finally, as if by magic,
As I turned one around
And tightened a twinkly light
Low to the ground...
A glimmer there appeared,
Much to my delight,
And the tree once more glowed
And was festive that night!
There was hugging and smiling
And much happiness too.
May all of your lights
Beam brightly for you!!

Tree-mendous Delight!

Christmas Glow

Oh, what if I had missed this glow
And of such beauty would never know?!
Thankfully, I did not miss the sight
Of your sweet face by candlelight.

Your face in innocence glows and shines,
As the light your face defines;
Each beam kisses your sweet face
And lingers there in sweet embrace.

The candle flame has done its part,
Reflecting in its tiny spark
The sweetness of your tender heart.
Never will I forget the sight
Of my sweet child by candlelight...

Christmas Palms

Sunny climate, warm and balmy,
Occasionally can be stormy ~~
But home to palms that shoot up tall
And don't change colors in the fall.

Trees with leaves that take up a branch,
Whose heart can be harvested for food,
But whose chances of being a good Christmas tree
Aren't very good.

There they stand, side by side,
Each splendid in its own way,
Making a great photo for my book
And a lovely memory of my Christmas Day.

It's Beginning to Look a Lot Like Christmas

Just before Christmas

Just before Christmas,
Our house is in a tizzy.
Everyone is working hard,
And everyone is busy!

Daddy is hanging lots of lights
Around the house outside.
And, once they all are working,
His face is filled with pride!

Mom is baking lots of goodies
And cleaning house from bottom to top.
You can slow her down, sometimes,
But you can't get her to stop!

Everything must be just perfect
'Cause company will be here right away,
And we want the house really festive
For the meal on Christmas Day!

Kids are getting anxious,
But staying out of the way,
For they don't want to jeopardize
The path of Santa's sleigh!

Yes, just before Christmas,
There's a lot of stuff to do
To create the kinds of memories
That will last a whole life through.

Make Way for Santa & His Sleigh

COOKING UP a JOLLY CHRISTMAS

Look at Him – He's a Gingerbread Man!

Look at him -- he's a gingerbread man!
Don't eat his feet, or he can't stand!
He has a little gingerbread wife,
And they live a tiny gingerbread life!

Little ginger kids keep popping out --
'Cause that's what gingerbread is all about!
Don't eat the ginger folks!
For they are too neat --

Don't eat their hands and don't eat their feet!
Just paint them over
And put them on your tree:
A cute little family for everyone to see!!

The Perfect Man

I have finally met the perfect man.
He's handsome as can be,
Is always dressed
In his very best:
A real delight to see!
He is always smiling
And never wears a frown.
I can take him anywhere.
And because he's made of gingerbread,
I'm always happy to share!

He's the Gingerbread Man

Christmas Cookies

We meet together just once a year
To bake gazillions of cookies
For those we hold dear...
Gingersnaps are a snap.
And mints are a breeze.
And Grandma's sugar cookies
Are guaranteed to please.
We bake through the day
And into the night
To make sure that the treats
Turn out just exactly right!
We cut out Christmas trees and angels and such,
Lovely tea cookies that melt to the touch!
What a lovely day or two or three
Creating treats for our family can be!
We get up on Christmas day,
Gathering up the happy sounds
Of thank-yous that come our way!

Love those Cookies!

I love the photos of us baking;
The kids are having such fun.
But the photo doesn't show
Just how much of the dough
Was in tummies
Before the baking was done!

Cookie Cutting is Lots of Fun,
and You Can Earn Lots of Dough!

Helping Mommy Bake for Christmas

I help Mommy at Christmas.
I love to help her bake.
She lets me lick the bowl
Of the goodies that we make.

Sometimes we bake cookies
And put chocolate chips inside.
I shape some that are tiny,
And some are very wide!

After the cookies are golden brown,
We take them out, and then
We put more dough on the sheet
And put it back again!

I love to eat the gooey dough,
And, sometimes, I'll agree
That more dough than goes into the oven
Goes inside of me!

The Taste of Christmas

Some people say that Christmas
Smells like cinnamon and spice,
While others say that turkey
Makes their homes smell nice.

But I love the smell of cookies,
As we bake them and then decorate.
To me, making cookies together
Gives Christmas its special taste!

Cookies for Santa and Presents for Me

Potato Candy for Christmas

We will make potato candy,
And eat it right away,
Not even saving much
To have for Christmas Day.

We boil a nice potato
And mix it with ease,
With powdered sugar and peanut butter ~~
A treat that's sure to please.

Mom said that when she was young,
It could be made very cheaply
But I love it just the same today,
And I eat until my tummy is filled completely!

Christmas Fudge

This is my year to learn to make
The fudge that is the gift we take
To friends and family when we go away
To visit them this holiday.

For years we have taken it with us,
And everyone always makes a fuss
Over what they say is a great treat,
Beautifully packaged and delicious to eat!

P.S. Hope you like the special wrap by (favorite candy bar)

Christmas in the Eyes of Children

Funny Food Christmas

When we get together with our friends,
On any holiday,
There are some favorite foods
That seem to come our way.

We always order pizza,
And we love chicken of any sort ~~
As long as we don't have to cook,
And the hubbies can watch sports.

The wives all get together
And make coffee and appetizers for all,
While the husbands are content with any sport
That involves some kind of ball!

It doesn't cost a lot of money,
But involves a lot of fun
To celebrate with our funny foods
Before the day is done.

Christmas Pizza

It may not be traditional,
But it is the tradition in our house
To have a Christmas pizza pie,
As we watch TV together,
For snuggling around the tree
Makes a good treat even better!

Making Merry

SECRET PALS and SECRET SANTAS

To My Secret Pal

The day is finally here
When I tell you who I am at last.
Hope you had a lot of fun.
The time went really fast!

You no longer have to wonder
About whom your "Santa" could be,
For I am here to tell you
That your Secret Santa is ME!

Dear Secret Santa Pal,
I've had a blast,
And who I really am
You get to know at last!

I guess you've wondered
Just who I am,
And you may be surprised to see
That, even though I said to you I wasn't...
Your Secret Santa is ME!

Dear Secret Santa Pal,
I've had a blast,
And now I will let you know
Who I am, at last!

I wish I could be there
Your surprise to see,
When I tell you that
Your Secret Santa was ME!

Yes, Virginia, There is a Santa Claus

Santa Surprise

Bet you didn't know,
Bet you couldn't guess
Who filled your mailbox
With scrapbook happiness!

Bet you had no inkling
Of whom your Santa could be.
I can finally tell you now:
Your Secret Pal was ME!

My name is _____,
And I was the friend
Who had the joy
Of getting to send
Little bits of fun your way
To brighten up
My Secret Pal's day!

Everyone has a secret pal.
The assignments have gone out.
Some of you have a guess,
But most are full of doubt.
The fun is in not knowing,
But having such a hint
As to from whom
Your packages were sent.
Have a fun experience,
And a laugh or two, as well.
And if you know someone else's pal,
Please do not tell.

We Believe in Santa!

LITTLE NOTES for CHRISTMAS CARDS

A Special Christmas Note

I know you have a special room to scrap,
But right now it's full of... stuff,
All tossed and tangled and spread about,
So you really can't turn pages out.

So as I pondered about a gift for you,
I knew exactly what I should do:
I'll offer my time and expertise
To bring order to your scraproom
And chaos to its knees!!

Just tell me the time
And pencil in the date,
And I'll be there to help.
Hooray! I just can't wait!!

Merry Christmas!!

Treasure

Treasure might be found
In a chest sunken underground...
Or treasure might be a part
Of treasured Christmas memories
Held in my heart...

*Snappin' & Scrappin'
Holiday Fun*

Christmas Jewels

Jewels may sparkle
Like the stars up above,
But nothing is as precious
As someone you love!

Christmas time brings out the magic
In the whole world around us,
As we become so aware of
The joy and happiness that has found us!

All that Glitters

All that glitters is not gold
Or even something
One can hold...
Glitter can come
From the Christmas sky
Or the sparkle of delight
In your baby's eye!

Come and celebrate with us
And help us trim the tree.
We want to share our happiness
With our friends and family!

Christmas comes but once a year,
And it gives us the chance to say
Wonderful things to friends we love,
Whether at home or far away.

The One True Christmas Gift

Merry Christmas from My Family

Merry Christmas from my family,
Whose faces are familiar to you all,
But who refused to pose for photos
When I asked them in the fall.

So with the blessing of my family
And the help of my PC,
You can see them as stick figures
On this card designed by me!

Here's a little card.
I made it for you myself.
I hope that it will cheer you
And make your day much brighter.
I was going to send a present,
But this card was so much lighter.

Merry Christmas and a Happy New Year!
I just wanted to say to you
That you are in my thoughts,
Each day the whole year through.

But sometimes we forget to say
To the people we love best
How happy they make our days
And how much our lives they've blessed!

There's No Time like the "Presents"

For Your Family

On this most special day of the year,
We want to share with those we hold dear
The joy, the peace and happiness
That comes from God above.
May you and your family be blessed by
The joy of knowing God's love.

A Blessed Christmas

May your Christmas be blessed
With joy and peace and happiness.
And may God's precious gift to you
Bless you today and the whole year through.

Celebrate

As we celebrate the birth
Of a tiny baby sent to earth,
We share our joy with those we love
And rejoice in God's greatest gift of love.

May His Peace surround you
And His Joy fill your day
And may this Christmas be wonderful
In every single way.

Joy to the World

SPECIAL CHRISTMAS EVENTS

The Christmas Play

We had a Christmas play
To celebrate the birth
Of precious Baby Jesus,
When God sent Him to earth.

I wanted to be an angel,
And brother wanted to be a sheep,
And our little baby sister
Crawled into the manger and went to sleep.

Mom was playing Mary,
And Dad was one of the kings,
With special gifts in his hands
That to Baby Jesus he would bring.

All in all it went real well ~~
Until the very end of the play,
When baby sister woke up in the manger
And ate a handful of the hay.

My Baby is in the Christmas Play.
She Can Hardly Wait
To Dress up in Angel Wings
And Tell of Christmas Day!

The Greatest Little Christmas Play Ever

The Pageant

The pageant got off to a very rough start
When the angels all wanted
To carry the harp.
The shepherds started sneezing
When we brought in the hay
In which the Baby Jesus would lay.
And one of the three kings lost his crown,
Which was nowhere to be found!
The little baby sheep had an accident,
Although we know it wasn't his intent...
And if you know what I mean
(And I think you do),
The baby playing Jesus had an accident too.

But when the curtain opened,
Like a bit of glory from above,
A hush fell over the crowd,
And we could feel God's love.
The shepherds stopped sneezing
(And we'll never know why).
The baby started cooing
From what had been a cry.
The king's crown appeared
(It had been in the car).
And we all gasped
At the sight of the star!

It was a glorious Christmas,
And it started that night.
For, in God's perfect timing,
It all turned out right!

Silent Night, Holy Night
His Love Shines Bright

Mommy's Little Angels

Look at my little girls,
Dressed in wings and curls,
Singing in an angel choir.
How precious is this sight,
Which brings me such delight
And fills my heart with joy!

Look at my little son,
My rough and tumble one,
Trying so hard his composure to keep ~~
When he really wants to pet the sheep!

And there is the baby in the manger,
With tiny feet kicking in the air,
Dressed in some designer duds
That I know the Christ Child didn't wear...

But it is the gospel story that matters,
And it fills me up to overflowing
With the peace of Christmas in my heart
And the truth of Christmas knowing!

Outdoor Christmas

When Christmas comes to our town,
It's still nice and warm and sunny.
We think swimming on Christmas Day
Is a lovely treat,
Though some may think it funny!

We see people packing turkey
To take it to the beach
For a picnic in the sun.
But Christmas holds the same joy
For each and every one!

Together for the Holidays

Four-Wheeler Christmas

We are moving now.
We are in style.
Got the four-wheelers
We've wanted for a while.

Gotta keep them clean
And in good shape,
So we can travel in style
When we need a break!

Love my four-wheeler.
It's a gift so neat.
Four wheels in the dirt
Sure have two-wheelers beat!

Baby's Christmas

The baby got a soft toy
And cooed sweetly in her seat,
As if she knew the reason
She received this lovely treat!

She was in the best of humor
And giggled all day long
And even seemed to join in
As we sang a Christmas song.

She had never seen a Christmas tree,
Until we brought it in the door,
And clapped her hands as we decorated it,
As if to request that we add more!

What joy babies brings to Christmas,
They add so much to the holiday ~~
As if they know that we are celebrating
A baby's birth on that first Christmas Day!

Winter Fun

Come and Meet Our New Son

We know you'd like to meet him,
And we won't keep you guessing.
We will formally present to you
Our little Christmas blessing!

We've set aside a special day,
Saved it especially for our honored guests.
Hope that you can come and visit,
After mommy and baby have their rest.

DATE
TIME
ETC.

Album for First Christmas

I knew it was something
I just had to do ~~
Creating this special
Little book for you ~~
So that you can understand,
In years to come,
That this first Christmas
Was a very special one!

Christmas and Babies

Oh What a Joy!

Bridal Shower at Christmas

It's really close to Christmas
And to the holiday,
But our friends are getting married,
And we want to send our love their way.

We invite you to come and join us.
We will have lots of fun
And think you will be glad you came
Before the day is done.

First Christmas Train

We took you to ride the Christmas train.
And the sparkles in your baby eyes
Were so wonderful to see,
As I held you in my arms,
And you rode the train with me!
Look at the smile on your sweet face.
Oh! I love that look!
Your tiny face looks like
A picture in a book!
Your little arms reaching out to us
For hugs and cuddles and such
Remind us of the Christmas joy
That we can hold and touch!
I've recorded this moment in my mind
And in my heart today.
This is a moment I'll treasure forever,
The memory of your first Christmas Day!

*The Magic of Christmas
The Wonder of Love*

Happy Christmas Birthday!

For folks who have birthdays at Christmas,
Things sometimes get lost in the rush
Of the holiday hustle and bustle,
And no one has time to make a fuss!

But no matter how busy we get
When the holiday is near,
Don't forget that we love you
And hold you very dear!

We may sometimes forget to throw a party
And send a Christmas card to say
That we wish you all the very best
On your very special day.

But this year we want to tell you,
In voices loud and strong,
That we love and appreciate you so much,
Today and all year long!

Have wonderful birthday!

P.S. You will receive a separate Christmas card!

A Christmas Wedding

We had a lovely holiday wedding
And thank you very much
For the lovely gift you sent.
It will be a treasure in our new home...
What a lovely sentiment!

A Christmas to Remember

First Christmas

Look at the sparkles in your eyes!
How wonderful to see,
As in awe and wonder,
You see the lighted Christmas tree!

Look at the smile on your sweet face.
Oh, I love that look!
Your tiny little face looks like
A picture in a book!

Your little arms reaching out to us,
For hugs and cuddles and such,
Remind us of the Christmas joy
That we can hold and touch!

Quite lovely for one to see
Are the lighted ornaments on our tree,
But better yet and more precious still
Is the precious face I see!

I've recorded this moment in my mind
And in my heart today.
This is a moment I'll treasure forever,
The memory of your first Christmas Day!

First Christmas as a Teen

This is the first Christmas
That you have been a teen
And not a young child
Or somewhere in between.

Have a Cool Yule

Dear Little One

Your very first Christmas
Is such a special day,
And I wanted to record it
In a very special way.

So I created this little book,
So that when you are older
You can look back and see
How special this day was
To your family!

Now I'm One

Look at me! Now I am one,
And my exciting life has really begun!
In this little book for the world to see
Are the firsts so special to me!

My first little tooth
Is recorded herein,
As well as my first little photo
And first little grin.

My first little haircut
With a tiny wisp of hair
And my first Christmas photo
Are here to share.

So many firsts have happened this year,
And so many wonderful things are here,
Recorded with love and tenderness too
In a book created in love to share with you!

Snow Babies First Christmas

Baby's First Christmas

What a wonderful day this will be!
Our family all gathered around
Baby's first Christmas tree!

The lights are lighted.
The decorations are hung.
The stockings are ready,
With one tiny one!

We have lots of tiny packages
With cute little toys.
Some are soft and chewy,
While others make noise.

We have waited forever
For this day to come,
For no Christmas is as special
As a baby's very first one.

Celebrating with Baby

It's your very first Christmas.
And right from the start,
We want it to be felt
Down deep in your heart.

Merry Christmas, Baby!

My December Birthday

It's such a special season ~~
I love this time of year!
I love the way folks celebrate
When my birthday is getting near.

The malls are full of goodies,
The radio plays carols all day long
And decorations are in the stores,
Almost before Thanksgiving is gone!

People are wrapping presents
And gathering up gifts to mail.
I can count on all of this excitement
Each December without fail.

I know it's for the Christmas holiday
That the excitement is underway,
But I love to pretend from time to time
That it's because it is also my birthday!

That's the fun of being born in December:
There is so much fun and celebration
That make it even more exciting
And fills me with exhilaration!

Christmas Birthday

What a wonderful day
To have a birthday!
It is very special indeed.
I wish you joy and happiness
And that in everything you succeed!
Happy Merry Birthday Christmas!!!

Anticipation

Happy Anniversary on Christmas

What a wonderful day to have an anniversary,
And what a wonderful day to celebrate!
We want to get this wish to you on time,
Wouldn't want it to be late!

Dear friends all come to mind,
As the holidays come into view,
And we want to celebrate the season
With each one of you.

We love the way we are reminded,
As we think of the two of you,
That it is time to celebrate the joy
Of your anniversary too.

We are sending you this little card
With the heartfelt wish inside
That you might be as much in love
As the day you were first groom and bride!

Christmas is a wonderful time of the year
To celebrate with all those we hold dear.
And what is more exciting than to say
"I do" on this wonderful holiday?

Our First Christmas

CHRISTMAS DECORATING

Choosing the Tree

I awoke this morning
Happy as could be
'Cause today is the day
We choose our tree!

We will all go together
And look until we drop
For a tree that will hold
Our angel at its top!

The tree must be special,
And it must be tall and strong
To stand inside our living room,
Guarding presents all month long!

So off we go to choose our tree.
Can you tell that I'm excited?
Can't wait until it's in our home ~~
Decorated, trimmed and lighted!!

My Favorite Tree

This is my favorite tree!
Of course, I say that every year.
But this time I really mean it,
For it is the best of all.
It takes up most of the room
And must be eight feet tall!

Searching for the Perfect Tree

Building a Tree

I never thought that I would see
My children build a Christmas tree.

A tree who may on Christmas wear
A star and icicles everywhere.

A tree that last year was put away,
But pulled out again for this holiday.

A tree that may be stored all nice and flat,
But fluffed out again as quick as that ~~

Under whose artificial limbs
Packages have rested, bearing children's whims.

Poems are written by moms like me,
When watching children "build their tree."

Underneath the Tree

Look at the children playing
Underneath the Christmas tree.
Someone grab the camera
And get that shot for me!

Look at the puppy staring
At the tree in awe.
I forgot this was the first
Tree he ever saw!

...and a Partridge in a Pear Tree

Who Says?

Who says that I can't be
Useful as a Christmas tree,
With decorations to adorn,
Tastefully chosen and well worn?

What have they brought here to stand
Beside my splendid, stately frame?
Some rather fragile evergreen ~~
I do not even know its name!

But wait! See how its branches smile
When balls and globes grace each.
And see how children laugh
When the lower ornaments they reach.

Perhaps there is room
For both of us in this fair space.
And maybe we can both have a share
In putting a smile on someone's face.

I will, in fact, be here
When this festive holiday is gone.
And even though my friend will be removed,
The memory will linger on.

Perhaps someone's eyes can see
Our beauty and take delight
In the palm and the evergreen, side by side,
And record it in a photograph tonight.

And years from now, they will again
Look at the two of us and remember.
Then they will grin,
Softly saying to themselves,
"Oh, I remember when."

Tropical Christmas

Christmas "Wrapture"

Oh, look! The tree is up.
That means that Christmas is coming.
Daddy is smiling ear to ear...
And Mommy is humming!

Oh, look! The lights are on the tree,
And the presents we are wrapping...
I think more presents appear
While we kids are napping!

Oh, look! The kitchen is getting busy.
Mommy is cleaning and cooking.
We see her sampling the food
When she thinks we aren't looking!

Oh look! The calendar says it's Christmas Eve,
And we are so excited.
We look forward to the morning.
I know we will be delighted!

Christmas "Wrap"

Look at all the lovely papers
Sitting on the shelf.
But I thought the wrapping
Was done by Santa's elf!

Rockin' Around the Christmas Tree

Poinsettia Passion

You usually don't see them
In the summer or the spring!
But when winter comes and snowflakes fall
And Christmas is around the bend,
Poinsettias pop up everywhere,
With each one having a twin!

You see them in the market.
You see them in the shops.
They are displayed everywhere
In big ceramic pots!

It makes my mom so happy,
When poinsettias are the fashion
Because her heart is filled
With such poinsettia passion!!

❧

Mommy's jobs were to cook and clean
And make sure Christmas was just right.
Daddy had one single job,
And that was the Christmas lights.

Christmas Eve so quickly came
And flowed without a hitch,
Except that there were no Christmas lights
When Daddy flipped the switch!

Deckin' the Halls with Love and Holly

Decorating for Christmas

Years come and go
So very fast,
But Christmas memories
Always last.

Mistletoe and shiny bells
(Hung on tree or post),
Hugs and kisses and teddy bears
Are some memories treasured most.

Little children trim the tree,
So happy with their task.
"When will Santa be here?"
Is the question that they ask.

Watching them as they laugh and play,
Underneath the family Christmas tree,
I realize with a happy heart
That I'm watching a treasured memory.

I'm Taking Photos...

Of the decorations on the Christmas tree,
Of the lights that twinkle so merrily,
Of the children playing,
Of the grandparents as they come in the door,
Of the turkey in the oven,
And, oh, so much more!

Tinsel and Trees
My Family and Me

THROUGH CHILDREN'S EYES

My Doll Dilemma

I got a bride doll for Christmas,
But I think she is too fine
To climb the trees with brother and me,
And maybe too refined!

My Raggedy Ann loves climbing,
While my Barbie prefers to drive
Along beside me in her special sports car ~~
Perhaps she could give the bride doll a ride!

My brother has a GI Joe,
And I think he is too rough,
Although my brother throws him about
And says Joes are really tough!

I doubt they will get married,
For dolls don't seem to age like us.
But if Barbie got married first,
My bride doll might make a fuss!

Too Old for Dolls!

I guess I'm too old for dolls.
Don't get me one this year,
(If I get another one,
The kids will laugh, I fear),
Although I shall miss the excitement
Of finding on Christmas Day
A brand new Christmas doll
With which to play!

Christmas Cuties

Baby Dolls

I need to buy a baby doll,
But I don't get to anymore.
And my heart aches so much,
When I see them at the store.

There are aisles and aisles of lovely babes,
Dressed in pink and blue ~~
Precious little newborn faces
That remind me of my baby too!

There are bride dolls and model dolls
And soft ones that are pillows
And dolls that are for display only,
With skirts of ribbons and billows!

There are dolls that walk,
If you hold them by the hand,
Right beside the ones that talk
(And you can actually understand!).

There must be a lot of moms
Who miss those doll buying days,
Whose baby girls are all grown up
And have put away those childhood ways.

I got my girl a designer purse.
And when I wrap it I shall hide
Something special for her to find:
This cute little dolly inside.

Are we there yet?
Is Christmas here?
I've been waiting
For a whole LONG year!

Have a Holly, "Dolly" Christmas!

What Can I Give My Teacher?

What can I give my teacher for Christmas
To show her she is special to me?
I want something pretty,
Something lovely to see.

What can I give to my teacher
To encourage her each day
And thank her for the special things
That I listen to her say?

I have made her a picture
And colored it with my new crayons ~~
I know it will special to her
Since it was created with my own hands.

The Perfect Tree

We found the perfect tree,
And it wasn't very hard.
The only problem is...
It's in the neighbor's yard!

I'm so sad and nothing can cheer me.
I would cry, but Santa might hear me.
We moved into an awful place.
Sure it looks great, but
THERE'S NO FIREPLACE!

You'd Better Not Pout!

Problems

I saw a kid crying at the mall
And asked what was the matter.
He said his daddy wouldn't buy
A great big, tall stepladder.

So how would Santa get to his roof,
If his sleigh stopped on the ground?
For, from all the pictures that he saw,
Santa Claus was big and round!

I used to believe in Santa Claus,
And I used to truly believe
That Santa brought elf-made toys
On his rounds for Christmas Eve.

But now that I am older
And much wiser than before ~~
I think that Santa orders from
A great big online store!!

I love to wait for Santa.
I watch the sky on Christmas Eve.
I thought I saw him once,
But it was a big ole jet.
I haven't given up,
Though I haven't seen him yet!

I'm Santa's Favorite

Ohhhh, Santa!

Oh, Santa! I am telling on my brother.
He is being bad to me.
It really is disgusting
And an awful sight to see!

He is doing gross things
Related to his nose.
I am such a lady
That I can't mention "those"!

He went into my room,
When I wasn't there,
And got icing from a cupcake
In my favorite dolly's hair!

He doesn't deserve a visit,
Santa, not from you,
Until he gives up those things
That bratty brothers love to do!

But if to leave something
For every kid you must,
I think a bit of coal would be nice ~~
Or maybe just the dust!

Santa came to our house
And left a lot of toys.
Some were quite lovely.
And others were for BOYS!!

Getting Nuttin' for Christmas

CHRISTMAS TITLES

- A Christmas To Remember
- All Hearts Come Home For Christmas
- All Is Calm, All Is Bright
- Almost Christmas
- Away In A Manger
- Believe
- Blessed is Best
- Christmas at Paw Paws
- Christmas In Love
- Christmas in the Eyes of Children
- Christmas Jammies
- Christmas Morning
- Christmas Tree Shopping
- Christmas Wrapture
- Glad Tidings We Bring!
- Hark The Herald Angles Sing
- Here We Come A-Caroling
- Home For The Holidays
- Jesus Is The Reason For The Season
- Jingle Bells
- Joy To The World
- Lets Leave Christ In Christmas
- Love Is The Light Of Christmas
- Making Merry
- Mistletoe Magic
- O' Christmas Tree
- O Holy Night
- Our Best Christmas Ever
- Our First Christmas Together
- Peace On Earth
- The Christmas I Remember Most
- The Magic Of Christmas
- The Night Before Christmas
- The Real Meaning of Christmas
- The Spirit Of Christmas Is Love
- The Twelve Days Of Christmas
- 'Tis The Season
- White Christmas

About the Author

In a poem of that same name in her first collection, "Where's Thena, I Need a Poem About..." the author answers that question...

"I have always known, without a doubt, Just who I was, and what I was about. I wanted to marry, a wonderful man, and have a child, to hold my hand. I wanted to write, the things deep in my heart, And to share God's love, I wanted to do my part.

Mother. Wife. Poet. Author. Friend. Mentor. Anyone who has ever met Thena Smith (in person or cyberspace) understands that she has surpassed the childhood vision of her life's goals. Born, raised and educated in western Kentucky, Thena's career as a published poet began early in her life. "I learned to write in the first grade, and reading and writing have been my passions since that age," she said. "I entered a poetry contest in the third grade and won. My little poem was published in the local paper. I have never gotten over the thrill and never shall."

Throughout her marriage, motherhood, and employment, Thena fulfilled her creative passion through writing, photography and scrap booking. She gained recognition for her poems and her design as a contributing columnist to the on line magazine, PC Crafter. Many scrap bookers came to know her through the online message boards, where they would reach her by asking, "Where's Thena, I need a poem about..."

That line became the inspiration and title for Thena's first book. The book was the brainstorm of author/publisher Linda LaTourelle, founder of Bluegrass Publishing and the best selling Ultimate Guide series and other books and products. Geographic opposites (Linda was raised in California, and now lives in Western Kentucky in the same community in which Thena was born.), Linda met Thena shortly after her first successful compilation "The Ultimate Guide to the Perfect Word."

"This book was always my dream," Thena said. "Thanks to Linda, who IS Bluegrass Publishing, it became a reality." However, Linda was not the first to suggest that Thena compile her poems into a book. "A few years ago, I was asked by a women's group I was visiting if there was a collection of my work available," she recalled. "I proceeded to produce an envelope, a napkin, a sales receipt and various other scraps of paper from my pocket. I told them that here is a collection of my work and there are many more!"

If you're wondering "Where's Thena?" now, you can be sure she's busy writing her next best seller or two. Actually, she's working on a list of books from A to Z! Thena currently has several books under her pen, with at least another library full to come.

If you'd like more information about all of Thena's works, please visit our website at:

www.bluegrasspublishing.com

INDEX

INDEX

INDEX

INDEX

Our Best Sellers

Ultimate Guide to the Perfect Word
Sold over 200,00 copies—352 pages

Ultimate Card - 2nd Edition
Verses for Every Occasion

Ultimate Kids (Birth-Preschool)
Ultimate Kids II (K-6th Grade)
The Ultimate Kids Collection

Where's Thena? I need a poem about...
Bestselling Poet Laureate of the Message Boards

Whispers
It's All About Love

What Can I Say?
Poetic Wordart

Boardsmartz and Taste of Paste
A Delightful Duo for Teachers and Educators

Letters to Heaven
Words of Comfort for the Grieving Soul

Color Made Easy
Misti Wrote the Book on Color!

C is for Christmas
Words to Decorate the Holidays

Visit our website: www.BluegrassPublishing.com

More Best Sellers

Pocketful of Poems
Tiny and Sweet Ready to Use Embellishments

The Whole Megillah
Poetry with a Jewish Flair

LoveLines WordArt CD
Embellishments at the Click of Your Mouse

Ultimate Sampler Word/Card
A Generous Sampling on CD

Ultimate Kids 1 & 2 Sampler
Quotes on C~D Ready to Use

Clear Quotes
WordArt Transparencies

Brit Wit
Beautiful Full Color Transparencies

Freebies For You

The Ultimate Line
Our Informative Newsletter & It's Free!

Contests for Our Bluegrass Family
That's You!

FREE DOWNLOADS Every Week

More Surprises Coming Soon...

Visit our website: www.BluegrassPublishing.com

A Few Words From Our On-Line Friends

Thena helps to decorate our life with beautiful words in which she blends so eloquently, warmly and passionately.
~Jeanette http://jeanettes.typepad.com/a_passion_for_scrapbookin/

I love Thena's books. Every poem says something that you can apply to a layout or card, and it's just that perfect touch. *~Rachel Houghton*

Thena's poetry is beautiful and always right on target. She takes the words that we would like to say and presents them to us in the most perfect way every time. I was looking for a poem about the way my son scrunches his nose sometimes and I found just the right thing in one of her books! She says the things that I want to put on my pages, just so much better! *~Maite*

Thena's poetry warms the souls of scrappers and nonscrappers alike. Her verses can bring a smile, a chuckle or a tear to the reader's eye...sometimes all at the same time! Thena is truly the poet laureate of the scrapbooking culture." ~Judge Lisa

You can always count on Thena to provide a thoughtful sentiment for any occasion. The beauty of her words are a perfect addition to many of my projects.
~Hugs from Karyn Terlecky

Thena's work is always touching and heartfelt. Perfect for any occasion!
~Jamie Tharpe

Whenever I get brain-tied for a sentiment to accompany a much loved photo I turn to Thena. Her poems describe my feelings when my words fail me. Be it happy or soulful Thena has a poem to bridge the gap. ~Francy Inman

I always find myself reaching for Thena's poetry to add just the right sentiment to my projects. She knows how to express the thoughts of my heart—I won't craft without her!
~Danielle Collins

With Thena's amazing creativity and sincere emotion put into writing, you will never again be at a loss for the perfect words! *~Jlyne Hanback*

This little thank you is just the start
of all the gratitude that's in my heart
~Thena

Thank You!

Thank you friends for reading
My poems and diddies, too.
It's been my greatest pleasure
To write this book for you!

Thank You, God,
For sending to me
A gift that means
eternity!

Bluegrass Publishing Inc
Mayfield, KY
270.251.3600
www.bluegrasspublishing.com

BLUEGRASS PUBLISHING ORDER FORM

me: _____

dress: _____

ail: _____

Date: _____

City/St/Zip: _____

Phone: (_____) _____-_____

PAYMENT INFORMATION

eck: (#_____) **Credit Card:** ☐ Visa ☐ Master Card ☐ Discover ☐ American Express   Security Code _____

Account Number _____-_____-_____-_____   Exp. Date ____-____ Name on Card _____

☐ **Check here to receive "The Ultimate Line" newsletter and promotional offers as they become available via your email.**

TOTAL $_____

#	DESCRIPTION	QTY	UNIT	TOTAL
	THE ULTIMATE LINE...			
	Ultimate Guide to the Perfect Word		19.95	
	Ultimate Card - 2nd Edition		19.95	
	Ultimate Kids (Birth-Preschool)		19.95	
	Ultimate Kids II (K-6th Grade)		19.95	
	Where's Thena? I need a poem about...		19.95	
	Whispers		12.95	
	What Can I Say?		12.95	
	Boardsmartz		14.95	
	Taste of Paste		14.95	
	Letters to Heaven		14.95	
	Color Made Easy - Color Palette * NEW		24.95	
	C is for Christmas —Words to Decorate...		14.95	
	The Whole Megillah (Scrapbooking Jewish)		12.95	
	Pocketful of Poems—Babies Vol 1		7.95	
	Pocketful of Poems—Toddlers Vol 2		7.95	
	Pocketful of Poems—Kids Inc. Vol 3		7.95	
	Pocketful of Poems—Teen Thing Vol 4		7.95	
Column One Total			**$**	

ITEM #	DESCRIPTION	QTY	UNIT	TOTAL
	DIGITAL CD'S & TRANSPARENCIES...			
	LoveLines CD		9.95	
	Ultimate Sampler Word and Card CD		9.95	
	Ultimate Sampler Kids 1 and 2 CD		9.95	
	Clear Quotes—School Days		2.25	
	Clear Quotes—LoveLines		2.25	
	Clear Quotes—Christmas		2.25	
	Clear Quotes—Autumn		2.25	
	Clear Quotes—Military		2.25	
	Clear Quotes—Baby Month by Month		2.25	
	Clear Quotes—Pets		2.25	
	Brit Wit - Treasures Deep		3.50	
	Brit Wit - Borders - Garden Party		3.50	
	Brit Wit - Borders - April Showers		3.50	
	Brit Wit - Borders - Seasons of the Year		3.50	
	Brit Wit - Borders - Sunset Serenade		3.50	

Shipping $2.95 for the first item and $1.00 each additional Book or CD

Total This Column	**$**
Total Column One	**$**
Kentucky 6% Tax (if applicable)	**$**
Shipping	**$**
TOTAL ORDER	**$**

* Call for quote on priority or international shipping

to if different than billing address:

ME: _____

DRESS: _____

Y/STATE/ZIP: _____

ONE : _____ CONTACT: _____

BP

Bluegrass Publishing, Inc.
PO Box 634 • Mayfield, KY 42066
(270) 251-3600 • Fax (270) 251-3603
www.BluegrassPublishing.com
E-mail: service@theultimateword.com